MW01245589

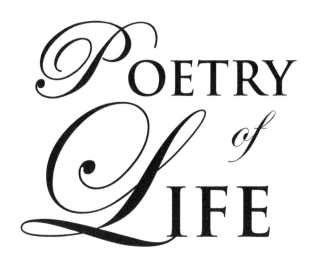

POETRY of LIFE

LOLA WAINWRIGHT-WANSLEY

Copyright © 2022 by Lola Wainwright-Wansley.

ISBN 978-1-958678-26-8 (softcover)
ISBN 978-1-958678-27-5 (ebook)

All rights reserved. No part of this book may be reproduced or transmitted in any form or by any means, electronic or mechanical, including photocopying, recording, or by any information storage and retrieval system without express written permission from the author, except in the case of brief quotations embodied in critical reviews and certain other noncommercial uses permitted by copyright law.

Printed in the United States of America.

Book Vine Press
2516 Highland Dr.
Palatine, IL 60067

CONTENTS

Introduction v

Winter 1

Sunshine 2

My pledge 3

Change 4

The Blue Prints 5

Sheltered life 7

Cry For the Homeless 8

Family Unit 10

Invisible Walls 12

$\mathscr{I}$NTRODUCTION

I have been inspired to write poetry for a number of years, my interest has taken me to materials, situations in life, people and their conditions, such as life situations, like being homeless, losing a job, these things are not to say they are conditions that will be permanent, but temporary, things that are repairable, there are ways to solve most issues that we as human beings come across on a daily basis.

As an Author, I tend to write when I am given different poems while riding along in my vehicle, I also wake up from sleep and from remembrance, I try and write what the Creator God has given me to say, I do not take total credit for my poems, I believe it is a gift that I have been given, and I want to share it with the world.

Most of my poems are written from my heart and soul, I want to bring to the audience, that while we are in this world, we can make the world a better place by contributions like, art, literature, writings, that can inspire the human experience that there is a bright side to things that can cause pain in life, and turn pain into a joyful situation, just because you have had some ups and downs in life, does not mean it will always be that way.

Learning how to think positive about things, and not negative, makes a big the difference, I found out that the spoken word began to form whatever we speak, so if I speak negative, it will form negative things, so I can do all things through Christ that strengthens me is better than saying, I will never have anything good in life, I would rather think positive, and call good for us, rather than call bad for us. Positive thinking.

Uplifting the hearts of people is what we intend to do as we write, from true experience, I can tell you it is better to build someone up than to tear them down, I get joy when I see a hungry person eating, a crying child comforted, a homeless person housed, a naked person clothed, a sick person healed, jobless person back into the workforce, temporary situations have remedies.

WINTER

The Mountains all covered
With pearly white snow,
People skiing
With faces aglow,
Laughing and making
Melody as they go,
Birds chirping,
Flying swiftly about,
I feel so wonderful I want to shout
What a beautiful day
As I look around,
Melting snow all over the ground,
I smell the freshness of winter
As the gentle breeze
Pass over my face,
I am so amazed at the
Beauty that surrounds me,
And thankful for this winter day,
For soon spring will chase the winter away.

Lola Wansley

Sunshine

There is something about
The sunshine breaking through
The clouds mask, and morning dew
All over the beautiful green grass,
Keep on shinning for me,
For when I see you peeping through
Those clouds, I will surely sing out loud.
With your bright glow
Everyone who sees you will know,
Darkness cannot remain
When the sun comes on the scene,
It goes away somewhere serene

Lola Wansley

My PLEDGE

I will never allow negative things
Said by others against me to stop my progress
I will never allow negative vibes
From others around me cause me to digress
When I am told I cannot do a thing,
That is when I will strive to do all I can,
I will look doubt in the face,
And I will say you are defeated until my plan
Is completed, I will not be cheated,
Instead of lying down on a comfortable bed,
I will accomplish whatever I said.
I will not allow others to do my thinking,
Any time I fall, I will get up and try again,
I intend to win, again and again.
I will walk like a winner, talk like a winner,
I will not allow a pretend tail to
Be tucked beneath me, for others to see,
I will be bold, level headed and sure,
That I am not giving up on myself, and no one else.
It is my pledge to the future.

Lola Wansley

CHANGE

I have learned to appreciate
The beauty of all the things
That surround me
From the grass that grows,
The air we breathe,
Even the smallest little tree,
The bugs the frogs,
The dogs, the hogs,
The crickets,
All of the animals that are alive,
They struggle to survive
I see change in a close range,
A babies cry to be changed,
Seeing a homeless person begging in the street,
Change it is not how things used to be,
Our cities are begging for change,
Our communities are not the same,
We need positive change,
I will do whatever I can to make a difference,
And create change,
I will redeem the time that have been lost,
And make every day count for something positive.

Lola Wansley

THE BLUE PRINTS

One day a Carpenter laid out the Blueprints
Of a different structure
That he was about to build
He loved his work so much,
It gave him such a thrill,
He never worried whether he would
Complete a structure or not,
The thought never entered his heart,
He knew in order to finish his work,
He must first make a start.

Some of the structures that the Carpenter built,
He sometimes took a loss,
Before the Carpenter set out to build,
He did not count up the cost.
He saw the joy it gave the folks who would dwell
Within, he soon forgot about his loss
And began to build again.
As the Carpenter followed the blueprints
He fastened the foundation on to the land,
You would have to be a builder, to really understand.
The Carpenter keeps the building, while the
Master holds his hand.

For the Carpenter takes all the negatives,
And turns them inside out,
And somehow they become positive,
Without the slightest doubt.
The Carpenter chose a trade
That will always be in demand
Whether he builds indoors or
Out on a plot of land.
Once you have met the Carpenter ,
This is what he will say,
Just take the blueprints
And follow them day by day,
Counting up the cost all along the way,
The Carpenter did not question
Every obstacle that stood in his way,
The challenge of building around
Them was the price he chose to pay,
It was the blueprints that taught the Carpenter
how to pray.

Lola Wansley

SHELTERED LIFE

Protection from the outside world,
Just a sort of Country girl,
No outside job, she stayed
At home, with no mind
Or intent to roam,
Watching the children as they played,
As she disciplined they obeyed.
The food was cooked,
The home was neat,
Dad could come home
And rest his feet,
And one day suddenly
Things began to change,
The sheltered life was rearranged,
There was no protection
From the outside world given to this country girl.

Lola Wansley

CRY FOR THE HOMELESS

In every city throughout our land,
You will see the homeless
Without stretched hands,
Some are asleep lying on the ground,
They have searched all night
For a place to lie down,
All their possessions are in a pack,
Some just have the clothes
That are on their backs,
Some have lost Mom and Dad,
Realizing that they were all that they had.
They have not got over their terrible loss,
Now all alone they must carry their cross.
Some are young, some are old,
Half the story have not been told,
Some are sick and destitute,
Many of their hearts now throb,
Some have even lost their jobs,
You are now hurting, look,
We see you old woman,
We see you old man,
It is you who have helped
To build this land,

Now you are homeless,

Oh what a mess
We have made,
Coming to you aide,
So reach out your hand,
There are places in this land
That can help you to dream
And live again,
You can trust them,
We know that if you were well,
You would not choose the streets to dwell,
So on the dark cold winter nights,
We want you tucked in bed real tight,
Not on a bus stop bench,
Or in a trench,
Or on a sidewalk, let's have a talk, at first,
There was one or two of you, homeless,
Now there are thousands, oh America, what shall
we do?

Lola Wansley

FAMILY UNIT

The family unit is becoming extinct,
separation and divorce
is on the brink,
somewhere there is a missing link,
either mom or dad has gone away,
and all the children have gone astray,
and where is the family unit today?
there is a price that one must pay,
it made the family become this way,
first we must find the missing link,
now sit me down and let me think,
I remember the love we once shared
back then I know we really cared,
money and materials did
not much matter,
it was the lack of love that
caused the family to shatter,
I will find a way and do it today
if it is love that the family lacks,
I will do what I can to bring love back,
removing the dust from my heart,
let this love now impart,
that was injured from the start,

love will mend all broken hearts
that was injured from the start, Mom and Dad
Sue and Jack, love have brought the family back.

Lola Wansley

INVISIBLE WALLS

While walls can be physical, tall,
Or strong, sometimes a wall
Is not where it belongs,
It can be big, and wide,
The house places where one can hide,
They can protect, and also block
They are open and they are locked
Walls separate, they divide,
There are spaces for people to hide,
You may not see the wall
With your naked eye,
But the wall is there so do not sigh,
The wall keeps people out are keep them inside,
Ignore them and you can survive.

Use the wall towards your success,
Just do not allow it to cause unrest,
People that you do not know,
Put up the wall as you go,
It is to protect you from a fall,
Yes sometimes we need a wall.

A wall can give shelter from the cold,
For the young or for the old.
The invisible wall cannot be seen,
It is inside our minds that is where it clings,
May I help you someone said,
I do not know you I am afraid,
I do not know you, my trust is thin,
The wall goes up, again and again,
Its invisible as I said,
The wall is there, it is in my head.

Lola Wansley